Library of
Davidson College

The Social Security Retirement Test
Right or Wrong?

Marshall R. Colberg

American Enterprise Institute for Public Policy Research
Washington, D.C.

Marshall R. Colberg is professor of economics at Florida State University.

Library of Congress Cataloging in Publication Data

Colberg, Marshall Rudolph, 1913–
    The social security retirement test.

    (AEI studies; 205)

    1. Old age pensions—United States. 2. Income—United States. I. Title.
    HD7106.U5C567   368.4'3'00973   78-15476
    ISBN 0-8447-3307-5

AEI Studies 205

© 1978 by American Enterprise Institute for Public Policy Research, Washington, D.C. Permission to quote from or reproduce materials in this publication is granted when due acknowledgment is made.
The views expressed in the publications of the American Enterprise Institute are those of the authors and do not necessarily reflect the views of the staff, advisory panels, officers, or trustees of AEI.

Printed in the United States of America

CONTENTS

INTRODUCTION

1 HISTORY OF THE RETIREMENT TEST 1

World War II 3
The Postwar Period 4
Annual Test Initiated 5
Later Changes 5
Automatic Adjustment of Test 8
The 1977 Amendments 9
Tabular History and Projection 9

2 SOME DETAILED CONSIDERATIONS IN THE RETIREMENT TEST 11

Cost of Living Differences 11
Cost Differences in Florida 11
Monthly Test: An Escape Clause 13
Annual Test May Help Beneficiary 15
Family Effects of Earnings Test 16
Retroactive Entitlement 16
Self-Employment 18
Some Further Legal Details 19

3 EARNED INCOME VERSUS PROPERTY INCOME 23

Human Capital 23
Earned Income and the Income Tax 25

Housewives' Services 25
  Civil Service Retirement System 27
  Military Pensions 27
  State and Local Plans 28
  Private Plans 28

4 RECOMMENDATIONS BY THE QUADRENNIAL ADVISORY COUNCIL ON SOCIAL SECURITY AND OTHERS 31

  The Position of the Social Security Administration 31
  Wallis Advisory Council Recommendation 32
  Hsaio Committee Recommendation 34
  Myers's Position on the Test 35
  Other Recommendations Regarding the Test 36
  Raising the Retirement Age 37
  Delayed Retirement Credit 38
  Retirement Test in Other Countries 39
  Recommendation of Committee for Economic Development 40

5 COST OF ELIMINATING THE TEST 41

  Real National Income 41
  Cost Estimates for the System 41
  Labor Supply in Theory 43
  Labor Force Participation 43
  Estimated Added Tax Collections 46

6 SUMMARY 47

APPENDIX 51

INTRODUCTION

One of the most controversial features of our social security system is the very high penalty placed on persons who have reached retirement age but are under a specified age (now seventy-two) and who earn income in excess of the permitted level. This penalty provision is variously known as the retirement test, the earnings test, the work-income test, the earnings limitation, or the work clause. By any name, the provision has always been the source of public complaint, legislative concern, and administrative difficulty.

The 1977 amendments to the Social Security Act made many important changes, including alteration of the retirement test, partly in the direction of making it less restrictive but partly in the opposite direction. To illuminate the nature and effects of the new provisions related to the earnings test, the present study will deal in some detail with the test as it existed in 1977 as well as with the latest revisions.

In 1977 retirement benefits were not withheld if earnings of an otherwise qualified individual did not exceed $3,000 for the year. The basic rule was a one dollar reduction in benefits for each two dollars earned above $3,000 for the year. No deduction from the social security check was made, however, for any month in which an employee earned $250 or less, regardless of annual income. Self-employed beneficiaries were required not to perform "substantial services" during a month. At age seventy-two the work-income test was no longer applicable.

The new legislation lowers to seventy the age at which persons may receive full benefits without regard to earnings, but this change does not become effective until 1982. It is not a very impressive liberalization, especially since the Social Security Administration, which has strongly supported the retirement test, itself recommended seventy as a suitable age for its termination over a quarter century ago (see Chapter 1).

Exempt annual earnings were raised to $4,000 in 1978, $4,500 in 1979, $5,000 in 1980, $5,500 in 1981, and $6,000 in 1982. The projected increase is much less impressive if the probability of substantial inflation is taken into account. For example, the present value of $6,000 that is four years away is only $4,410 at an 8 percent discount rate. Consequently, the real earnings limit (in 1978 dollars) will be raised only from $4,000 to $4,410 if an 8 percent inflation rate persists over the 1978–1982 period.

The liberalization of the annual income test for the year 1978 was more substantial. An important move in the opposite direction was also made, however, in that the monthly test was abolished except for the year of initial retirement. In my opinion this was a socially unfortunate action, for reasons that will be indicated in Chapter 2.

Another change made by the 1977 amendments that seems sure to generate much complaint was a provision that discriminates against beneficiaries under sixty-five years of age. They are allowed annual earnings of $3,240 in 1978 with automatic adjustments after that. Since the automatic adjustments are likely to be somewhat less than $500 per year, beneficiaries under age sixty-five will probably be subjected to an increasingly tight squeeze on permitted earnings compared with the older group.

This squeeze on younger beneficiaries is in line with (but not necessarily justified by) the desire of Congress to defer the typical retirement age. In order further to reduce the desirability of retirement before sixty-five, the 1977 amendments reduced the cost-of-living adjustment for early retirees. Prior to the new law, the cost-of-living adjustments in the benefits of those who retired early were based on a calculation of benefits they would have received if they had not retired early. Now the cost-of-living increases of these persons will be based instead on their reduced benefits. (With retirement at age sixty-two benefits are reduced by 20 percent of those paid for retirement at sixty-five.) Some other changes made by Congress in the 1977 amendments to the Social Security Act that have some relation to the retirement test will be mentioned in the following chapters, as will special problems related to self-employment.

The social security system of the United States has been increasingly investigated in recent years because of its vast size and importance, and some of the recommendations have been incorporated into law (for better or worse). The present booklet will concentrate on only one important subject—the retirement test related to old-age and survivors insurance (OASI).

1
History of the Retirement Test

The Social Security Act was signed by President Franklin D. Roosevelt on August 14, 1935. A fairly close link between benefits and earnings was specified, with old-age benefits computed on the basis of total wages earned by the individual from covered employment after December 31, 1936, and before age sixty-five. Only $3,000 per year in earnings was counted in both the collection of payroll taxes and the computation of annuities. Benefits were to start in January 1942, but the date was advanced to January 1940 by amendments enacted in August 1939.[1]

During the early years of social security, the insurance aspect of old-age benefits was stressed. In fact, it was to be the "world's largest insurance system."[2] The Social Security Board also wrote that "the system was built to a considerable extent on principles of individual savings and on certain traditions of private insurance practice."[3] According to Eveline M. Burns, the insurance idea was important to the adoption of the program, "because its apparent analogy with private insurance made the change acceptable to a society which was dominated by business ethics and which stressed individual economic responsibility."[4]

In spite of the implication that old-age benefits were payable as a matter of right because of workers' accumulated contributions to a fund, the original Social Security Act required complete forfeiture of

---

[1] *First Annual Report of the Social Security Board, 1936* (Washington, D.C., 1937), p. 19.
[2] *Second Annual Report of the Social Security Board, 1937*, p. 12.
[3] *Fourth Annual Report of the Social Security Board, 1939*, p. 35.
[4] Eveline M. Burns, "Social Insurance in Evolution," *American Economic Review*, Supplement, vol. 34, pt. 2 (March 1944), p. 199.

benefits in any month when there was any work in covered employment. (Uncovered fields included agricultural and domestic employment, public employment, self-employment, and work for nonprofit institutions.)

The 1939 amendments to the Social Security Act eliminated the original guarantee that a worker or his estate would receive not less than his own contribution, weakened the principle of individual equity, and moved the system more in the direction of an institution for the redistribution of income. The ambivalence of goals has affected many facets of social security, including attitudes toward the retirement test. Those who think of the program primarily as a device for the annual redistribution of income tend to favor a strict earnings test so that benefits do not go to persons with large earned incomes. Those for whom social security is primarily a compulsory saving program see no need for a retirement test since they regard government annuities as an alternative to private annuities that can be received regardless of other income. It is also important how workers perceive their social security "contributions."[5] To the extent the social security levy is considered to be just another tax that reduces take-home pay, the effect will be to discourage labor force participation, especially by secondary workers; to the extent the tax is clearly identified as saving, workers may consider the tax as part of their wage, largely eliminating distortions in work effort.[6]

Paul H. Douglas, an important consultant on social security during the 1930s, professor of economics at the University of Chicago, and later a United States senator who helped shape amendments to the law, wrote:

> This requirement that the aged must leave regular jobs in order to obtain their annuities was undoubtedly dictated by two sets of considerations. The first was that those who had regular jobs would not be in need of annuities, while the second was a desire to clear the labor market of the older employees in order to make a place for the unemployed young workers.
>
> This provision, however, is in part a confusion of the idea of relief with that of insurance. The workers will have made direct contributions for half of their annuities and in-

---

[5] Milton Friedman, "Payroll Taxes, No; General Revenues, Yes," in Michael J. Boskin, ed., *The Crisis in Social Security* (San Francisco: Institute for Contemporary Studies, 1977), p. 25. Friedman notes that the term "contribution" is wholly misleading for a tax and that the "trust fund" is really a petty cash fund.

[6] This point is made by Alicia H. Munnell, *The Future of Social Security* (Washington, D.C.: The Brookings Institution, 1977), p. 41.

directly will have paid for most of the employers' contributions as well. When the system is thoroughly established, they will therefore have earned their annuities. To require them to give up gainful employment is, in reality, attaching a condition upon insurance which they have themselves bought.

This provision will also be difficult to enforce. For, strictly interpreted, it would prevent an aged person from keeping a small shop or operating a farm. All sorts of difficulties will arise in the attempt to ferret out such facts and to keep those over the age of sixty-five from having some gainful job.[7]

Writing in 1936, Douglas put his finger on the basic problem—annuities versus income redistribution—that has always caused difficulty and contention. His view on the ultimate incidence of payroll taxes is similar to present-day opinion on the subject.[8]

The requirement of complete forfeiture of benefits in any month when there was any work in covered employment was only slightly liberalized in the 1939 amendments. Forfeiture of the entire benefit was then required for any month in which an individual rendered services in covered employment for wages of $15 or more. This was sometimes an implicit tax of more than 100 percent on wages, since the average primary benefit during the first six months of payments, January through June 1940, was $18.75.[9]

World War II

This harsh retirement test was continued through the years of World War II when many beneficiaries returned to covered employment and when it was far easier to earn $15 a month or more in part-time work. Any benefits received by a wife aged sixty-five or more were also suspended if payments to the primary beneficiary were disallowed. The earnings test was clearly not in keeping with an all-out war effort. The arguments of the depression era still prevailed, and it was thought that jobs needed to be opened up for young persons—even though they were rapidly being drafted into military service. The "lump of labor fallacy" apparently continued to dominate congressional thinking even in wartime when it was at its most fallacious!

---

[7] Paul H. Douglas, *Social Security in the United States* (New York: Whittlesey House, McGraw-Hill, 1936), pp. 171–72.
[8] See, for example, George F. Break, "Social Security as a Tax," in *The Crisis in Social Security*, p. 113.
[9] *Fifth Annual Report of the Social Security Board*, 1940, p. 35.

The Social Security Board itself regularly asked for liberalization of the retirement test, especially for elimination of the complete suspension of benefits in any month when earnings exceeded $14.99. In 1945 the board suggested that earnings of $25 or $30 per month be permitted without suspension of benefits. This was indeed a modest suggestion, but Congress did not act on it.

A stiff penalty existed for knowing failure by beneficiaries to report covered earnings of $15 a month or more. An additional month's benefits were suspended for each month of nonreporting, so that two months without benefits could result from each month of willful failure to report. In the words of the board: "Many beneficiaries are never able to resolve the double deductions and get back on the benefit rolls. If they work, no benefits are payable and no credit is received toward the accrued deductions. If they do not work, they have no means of subsistence."[10]

The Postwar Period

After World War II, the Social Security Administration continued to be extremely conservative in its recommendations regarding the retirement test. In its annual reports for 1948 and 1949, the administration recommended that permitted monthly earnings be raised from the $15 level to $50, but it still wanted benefits to be completely withdrawn for any month in which this figure was exceeded. In 1948 the Advisory Council on Social Security recommended a plan for reducing benefits by the amount that earnings exceeded the exempt amount. Although this plan amounted to a 100 percent implicit tax on excess earnings up to the total amount of social security benefits, it would have prevented a reduction in net cash flow to the beneficiary when earned income was only a little above the allowed amount. The Social Security Administration did not approve the plan, however, because it felt that the "administrative costs of such a plan would probably be disproportionate to the advantages gained."[11] The welfare of the agency itself, rather than the social welfare, appeared to be the primary consideration.

In 1950 Congress passed, and President Truman signed, substantial amendments to the Social Security Act in Public Law 734. Allowable monthly earnings were raised to $50, and the retirement test was eliminated at age seventy-five. (The Social Security Administration

---

[10] *Annual Report of the Federal Security Agency, 1945* (Washington, D.C., 1946), p. 401.

[11] *Annual Report of the Federal Security Agency, 1948, 1949,* p. 107.

had recommended that it be eliminated at age seventy.) Two years later earnings of $75 per month in covered employment were allowed. The test was still on only a monthly basis, so that large losses in monthly benefits resulted if earned income was above the limit in some months even if well below the limit in others.

Annual Test Initiated

An annual limit on earnings was introduced in 1955 when legislation signed by President Eisenhower came into effect. Earnings in both covered and uncovered employment were limited to $1,200 a year. (For self-employed persons, annual earnings of $600 in 1951 and $900 in 1953 were considered to be evidence of substantial gainful services.) For each $80 or fraction thereof over $1,200 annually there was a loss of one month's benefit, but a beneficiary could be paid for any month in which only $80 or less was earned, regardless of annual income. This provision was especially helpful to workers who retired toward the middle of a year in which preretirement earnings were relatively large. (Beneficiaries residing in foreign countries would have their benefits suspended for any month in which they worked seven or more days. This was a rough solution to the otherwise difficult problem of converting dollar limitations into foreign equivalents for a large number of currencies and with fluctuating exchange rates.) In 1959 the monthly limit on earned income was raised to $100.

Later Changes

A somewhat improved formula was legislated in 1960. The Senate voted to increase the yearly earnings limitation to $1,800, but a compromise with the House was necessary and a Conference Committee was appointed.[12] A rather strange formula resulted, effective in 1961, in which $1 of benefits was withheld for every $2 earned in excess of $1,200 up through $1,500 a year. The latter figure was increased to $1,700 by 1961 legislation, effective retroactively for 1961. For more than $1,700 the implicit tax rate was 100 percent on extra dollars earned. The monthly unpenalized pay remained at $100.

The increasing seriousness of the problem of inflation was recognized by the legislative and executive branches in the 1960s by two more upward adjustments in the earnings test, both of which retained

---

[12] Robert B. Stevens, ed., *Statutory History of the United States: Income Security* (New York: Chelsea House Publishers and McGraw-Hill, 1970), p. 584.

TABLE 1
Social Security Earnings Test, 1940–1982

Year First Effective	Dollar Amount Permitted without Reduction		Benefit Reduction	Age at Which Restriction Ends	Remarks
	Annual	Monthly[a]			
1940	—	14.99	Full monthly benefit	None	
1951	600[b]	50.00	Full monthly benefit	75	
1953	900[b]	75.00	Full monthly benefit	75	
1955	1,200	80.00	One month's benefit for each $80 or fraction over $1,200	72	All earnings covered[c]
1959	1,200	100.00	One month's benefit for each $100 or fraction over $1,200	72	
1961	1,200	100.00	$1 for each $2 of earnings from $1,201 to $1,700; $1 for each $1 of earnings over $1,700	72	As legislated in 1961 and effective retroactively for 1961
1966	1,500	125.00	$1 for each $2 of earnings from $1,501 to $2,700; $1 for each $1 of earnings over $2,700	72	
1968	1,680	140.00	$1 for each $2 of earnings from $1,681 to $2,880; $1 for each $1 of earnings over $2,880	72	

Year	Exempt amount	Reduction	Age	Notes
1973	2,100	175.00	$1 for each $2 of earnings over $2,100	72	Earnings in and after month of attainment of age 72 excluded
1974	2,400	200.00	$1 for each $2 of earnings over $2,400	72	
1975[d]	2,520	210.00	$1 for each $2 of earnings over $2,520	72	Indexing of permitted amounts initiated
1976[d]	2,760	230.00	$1 for each $2 of earnings over $2,760	72	
1977[d]	3,000	250.00	$1 for each $2 of earnings over $3,000	72	
1978	4,000	334.00	$1 for each $2 of earnings over $4,000	72	Monthly test applicable only in first year of retirement
1979	4,500	375.00	$1 for each $2 of earnings over $4,500	72	
1980	5,000	417.00	$1 for each $2 of earnings over $5,000	72	
1981	5,500	458.00	$1 for each $2 of earnings over $5,500	72	
1982	6,000	500.00	$1 for each $2 of earnings over $6,000	70	

[a] For self-employed persons dollar monthly limits on earnings were not specified, but "substantial services" were not permitted.
[b] Self-employment income only.
[c] Beneficiaries residing in foreign countries allowed to work up to seven days a month.
[d] Exempt amount determined by the Department of Health, Education, and Welfare under a wage-indexing formula.

SOURCE: *Social Security Bulletin, Annual Statistical Supplement, 1973*, p. 26, and other issues of *Social Security Bulletin*.

the extreme dollar-for-dollar penalty above a specified limit: $2,700 in 1966, and $2,880 in 1968. The penalty of $1 lost for $2 earned applied to earned income of $1,201 to $1,700 in 1961–1965; from $1,501 to $2,700 in 1966–1967; and from $1,681 to $2,880 in 1968–1972. The monthly income test, which was $100 from 1959 to 1965, was raised to $125 in 1966 and to $140 in 1968.

The incentive-killing dollar-for-dollar penalty was finally abolished in 1972, and the somewhat improved present formula of $1 lost for $2 earned was adopted, effective in 1973. Annual and monthly limits were placed at $2,100 and $175 respectively. Permitted yearly earnings without the $1-for-$2 penalty rose to $2,400 in 1974, to $2,520 in 1975, to $2,760 in 1976, and to $3,000 in 1977. Permitted monthly earnings rose to $200 in 1974, to $210 in 1975, to $230 in 1976, and to $250 in 1977.

Automatic Adjustment of Test

The unpenalized earnings permitted for 1975–1977 were determined by a more or less automatic adjustment process that has been described in the *Social Security Bulletin*:

> In 1974—and every year thereafter, whenever a "cost of living" benefit increase is established—a determination will be made as to whether an adjustment in the amount of earnings permitted without reduction in benefits is required. The determination is made by multiplying the monthly exempt amount in effect by the ratio of the average taxable wages (under the Social Security program) of all employees as reported in the first quarter of the calendar year of determination as reported for the latest [sic] of (a) the first calendar quarter of 1973 or (b) the first calendar quarter of the year in which the last automatic determination was made that resulted in an increase in the monthly exempt amount or of the year in which the monthly exempt amount was enacted.
>
> The product, rounded to the nearest multiple of ten dollars, will be the new monthly exempt amount effective with respect to the taxable years.[13]

The adjustment calls for an annual test of twelve times the monthly test. In short, permitted earnings were indexed by changes in average wage rates, which should allow for economic growth as well as for price inflation.

---

[13] *Social Security Bulletin, Annual Statistical Supplement*, 1973, p. 25.

The 1977 Amendments

Automatic adjustment has become somewhat less important since the 1977 amendments to the Social Security Act, which legislate $500 increments to the annual exempt amount for each year from 1979 to 1982, along with an increase to $4,000 for 1978. Automatic adjustment is specified after 1982, however, and it still applies to beneficiaries under age sixty-five, who will be able to earn $3,240 without penalty in 1978. As already mentioned, this discrimination against persons who accepted the popular option of early retirement is certain to be a source of much complaint. In my opinion no difference in the earnings test should exist for early retirees.

Tabular History and Projection

A tabular history and projection of the earnings test is shown in Table 1, beginning with 1940 when benefits were first paid. Table 2 shows that the monthly earnings test approximately doubled in terms of purchasing power between 1950 and 1973. The purchasing power

TABLE 2

Monthly Earnings Test in Real Terms, 1950–1977

Year	Nominal Test[a] (dollars)	Consumer Price Index[b] (1967 = 100)	Real Test[c] (dollars)
1950	50	72.1	69
1952	75	79.5	94
1954	80	80.5	99
1958	100	86.6	115
1960	100	88.7	113
1961	100	89.6	112
1965	125	94.5	131
1967	140	100.0	140
1972	175	125.3	140
1973	200	133.1	150
1975	210	161.2	130
1976	230	170.5	135
1977	250	179.6[d]	139

[a] See Table 1.
[b] U.S. Bureau of the Census, *Statistical Abstract of the United States, 1976* (Washington, D.C., 1976), p. 439.
[c] Nominal test divided by consumer price index.
[d] Index for April 1977, *Monthly Labor Review*, vol. 100 (December 1977), p. 106.

of permitted monthly earnings declined considerably in 1975, however, when automatic adjustment of the test was begun, and rose only slightly in 1976 and 1977. Although the adjustment formula should provide for both economic growth and inflation, it did not provide even for the latter alone. Although the monthly test was abolished for 1978 (except for year of retirement), the monthly real equivalent of the new annual test would rise from an index number of 139 in 1977 to 172 in 1978 with an 8 percent annual inflation rate.

2
Some Detailed Considerations in the Retirement Test

Administration of most government programs at all levels—federal, regional, state, and local—requires the use of measures and formulas that are never fully appropriate to the activity and may be seriously inefficient and inequitable. The great financial importance of social security and its effect on almost everyone in the nation give its specific formulas an unusual significance, including those connected with the earnings test.

Cost of Living Differences

An obvious shortcoming of the retirement test is that it is uniform in nominal terms throughout the United States. This makes it substantially different in real terms from place to place. The dimensions of this problem are indicated by a comparison of costs for a retired couple in different urban locations shown in Table 3. The data apply to couples in which the husband is sixty-five years of age and older. According to these data, living costs are roughly 30 percent higher in Boston, the New York City area, and Honolulu than in Baton Rouge and Austin—and they are even higher in Alaska. Even greater differences exist between many rural locations, especially in the South, and the high-cost urban centers.

Cost Differences in Florida

Even within a single state, the cost of living may vary considerably from place to place. An important retirement state, Florida, now regularly measures price level differentials among counties. This Florida price level index does not measure the relative cost of living

11

TABLE 3

COST OF LIVING FOR A RETIRED COUPLE, 1975

Place	Cost per Year[a] (dollars)	Cost Index
Urban United States	6,465	100
Nonmetropolitan areas	5,728	89
Cities		
Austin, Texas	5,998	91
Baton Rouge, Louisiana	5,758	89
Boston, Massachusetts	7,575	117
New York City and northeastern New Jersey	7,540	117
Honolulu, Hawaii	7,339	114
Chicago and northwestern Indiana	6,464	100
Los Angeles and Long Beach, California	6,488	100

[a] For couples in which the husband is aged sixty-five or older.
SOURCE: U.S. Bureau of the Census, *Statistical Abstract of the United States, 1976* (Washington, D.C., 1976), p. 444.

for typical residents because the standard of living varies in different places. Still, it indicates in which counties the retirement test is relatively more burdensome because prices paid by residents are higher. Since the "market basket" is held constant, the indexes reflect differences in dollar outlays needed to buy this particular assortment of goods, housing, apparel, transportation, and health, recreational, and personal services in the various counties.[1] It can be seen in Table 4 that prices are more than 20 percent higher in the highest cost counties of southern Florida than in the lowest cost counties of northern Florida. The social security limitation on earnings therefore is more stringent in the former, where the number of social security recipients is especially large.

The political and statistical problems of introducing a test based on real earnings clearly would be extremely difficult, even if some broad differentiation were made between, say, urban and nonurban areas. Among the many problems would be that people often work in areas different from those in which they reside. But in the present earnings test the inequities among places with differing living costs

---

[1] The market basket is based on an in-depth consumer expenditure survey of Orlando, Florida, by the Bureau of Labor Statistics.

TABLE 4

Florida Price Level Index, October 1975
(Population-Weighted; State Average = 100)

Seven Highest Counties (southern Florida)	Index	Seven Lowest Counties (northern Florida)	Index
Monroe	109.26	Taylor	92.15
Dade	107.39	Putnam	91.82
Palm Beach	104.42	Osceola	91.31
Broward	104.02	Lafayette	91.24
Flagler	103.74	Washington	90.71
Collier	103.56	Suwanee	90.07
Martin	103.48	Holmes	89.62

Source: State of Florida, Department of Administration, Economic and Tax Research Unit, *Florida Price Level Index* (Tallahassee, 1976), p. 8.

illustrate well the compromise that is usually made between administrative feasibility and equity.

Retirement benefits themselves are less subject to the effects of location on real and nominal value. Average monthly earnings on which benefits are based should correlate positively with cost of living at the place of work. (Retirees have, of course, a substantial incentive to move to areas where the cost of living is relatively low, including some foreign countries.) The maximum death benefit of $255 in effect since 1954 is, however, quite different in real terms from one location to another, resembling the retirement test in this regard.[2]

Monthy Test: An Escape Clause

So long as there is an annual earnings test it is important to have a monthly test during the first year of retirement. Otherwise, for many persons, the entire flow of income would cease abruptly upon retirement, since their earnings for that year would already have exceeded the amount permitted without penalty. The 1977 amendments to the Social Security Act retained the monthly test for the first calendar year of retirement but eliminated it for subsequent years.

Prior to this legislative change there were situations considered as "abuses," especially by persons who regard social security old-age

---

[2] Alicia H. Munnell, *The Future of Social Security* (Washington, D.C.: The Brookings Institution, 1977), pp. 177–78.

benefits more as a form of relief than as annuities purchased from the federal government. In 1977, for example, if university and college professors, high school and elementary school teachers, and others on nine- or ten-month contracts were otherwise eligible for social security retirement benefits, they could receive such benefits during the vacation months, provided earned income did not exceed $250 a month.

The monthly test before 1978 also favored workers with irregular incomes. Take the case of an eligible person who received monthly benefits of $300 and who earned $240 a month for the first eleven months of 1977 but earned $4,000 in December. If, in his required April 1977 report to the Social Security Administration he had anticipated earning $240 in each of the twelve months, no benefits would have been withheld. In April 1978 he would report the year's income as:

1977 earned income	$6,640
Annual earnings test	$3,000
Excess earnings	$3,640

Instead of paying back $1,820 (half of $3,640) to the Social Security Administration as would seem to be required by the annual test, he would repay only the December benefit of $300. He would be entitled to keep the checks for all eleven months in which income was not over $250. If the $6,640 had been earned at a steady monthly rate of $553.33, the annual earnings test would have applied fully, and $1,820 in benefits would have been lost through withholding of checks. The beneficiary would thus gain $1,520 from the assumed irregularity of income, compared with regular monthly earnings.

An individual who anticipated earning $240 in every month of 1977 but who actually earned $4,000 in December, might well be questioned by the Social Security office. He could be called upon to prove that the large December earnings were actually payment for work during that month. He might also be asked why these large earnings were not anticipated in April 1977 when his report of expected earnings was due. Anticipations are fragile things, however, and he would probably not be penalized for what might be an honest mistake. Among retired professional persons, it is quite common to earn substantial consulting fees in a single month, and these may be difficult to predict.

The Social Security Administration has quasi-judicial power in various matters, including administration of the earnings test. If a beneficiary has been paid too much, there is ample room to forgive him and not recover the overpayment. If recovery "would defeat the purpose of the program" or "be against equity and good conscience," or if the recipient (including a survivor) is "without fault," repayment may be waived.[3]

Similarly, the monthly test was favorable to those entitled to retirement benefits who work in construction, agriculture, some tourism-related jobs, and other occupations with a strong seasonal element. The low off-season monthly earnings would likely have qualified such workers for some social security checks even if total 1977 income were far above $3,000. Where skill requirements are high, the short-run supply of qualified persons is quite inelastic (as is the case with many construction workers), and the pay rate during the normal working season is relatively high because of the seasonality of employment. But during the off-season workers may qualify for social security benefits under the monthly test and thus achieve a total annual income higher than would be possible in employment that is less seasonal.

In theory this social security bonus to irregularity would tend slightly to depress competitive wage rates in fields where the bonus is collected. Probably relatively few workers, however, are both entitled to benefits and aware that they can be collected. Some firms with irregular employment (for example, manufacturers of lamps on special orders) find it economical to hire older persons who can be laid off in slack months and draw social security benefits. This tendency would be greater if there were no retirement test at all, but under present conditions it is an argument in favor of the monthly test over the annual test.[4]

Annual Test May Help Beneficiary

Although the annual earnings test may serve as the base above which the present-day rule of $1 penalty for $2 earned applies, it can also serve to increase benefits. Under certain conditions benefits might be larger than they would be if there were only a monthly test (though not in comparison with no test at all). If an eligible individual in 1977 earned $300 per month in eight months but only $100 per month in

---

[3] U.S. Department of Health, Education, and Welfare, Social Security Administration, *Social Security Handbook*, 5th ed., Publication no. (SSA) 73-10135 (Washington, D.C., 1974), p. 325.

[4] A preference for employment of retired workers in some plants where skilled persons are needed but irregular work is offered was noted in M. L. Greenhut and M. R. Colberg, *Factors in the Location of Florida Industry*, Study no. 36 (Tallahassee: Florida State University, 1962).

four months, his yearly earnings of $2,800 would be below the permitted $3,000. He could therefore have collected monthly benefits for all months of the year.

Family Effects of Earnings Test

The annual retirement test is often called an implicit tax of 50 percent on earnings over the permitted amount. It can also cause unexpected suspension of benefits that are being received by other family members such as a wife or child. Excess earnings of the insured person are charged against the total monthly family benefit.[5]

Excess earnings of a second family worker or survivor (such as a wife, child, or widow) are charged only against the second family worker's or survivor's own monthly benefit. If both the insured person and other family members have excess earnings, the insured person's excess earnings are charged against the total family benefits payable on his record. Next, excess earnings of the second family worker are charged against his or her own benefits, but only to the extent that these have not already been charged with the insured person's excess earnings.[6]

Retroactive Entitlement

The Social Security Act permits eligible persons to obtain retroactive benefits for as much as twelve months before the month of application. Many persons have chosen this option in order to receive a relatively large lump sum. For example, in 1977 a person retiring in the month he attained age sixty-five could receive twelve months of retroactive benefits if the earnings test did not prevent it. His or her ongoing benefit would, however, be reduced by 6.66 percent.[7]

Beginning in 1956 for women and 1961 for men, permanently reduced benefits were made available at age sixty-two. The option has proved to be very attractive. According to a survey by the Social Security Administration of the entire group of 1,157,000 persons receiving retirement benefits between July 1968 and December 1969, more than half claimed retroactive entitlement, and more than a third

---

[5] *Social Security Handbook*, p. 292.

[6] *Social Security Handbook*, pp. 292–93. This publication continues to use the term "insured" despite the departure from the original "insurance" concept.

[7] Robert J. Myers, "Social Security Financial Woes Substantially Solved," *Quarterly Newsletter* of Edward H. Friend and Company, Washington, D.C., vol. 2, no. 4 (Winter 1977–1978).

claimed the maximum of twelve months' retroactivity.[8] Often retroactive benefits were claimed at age sixty-two. More women than men elect early retirement, perhaps because they can more easily adjust their hours of work to meet the earnings test. Also, if her husband has not yet retired, a wife with a sufficient work history can claim benefits at age sixty-two. Later, she may be eligible for larger benefits based on her husband's work record.

The possibility of claiming up to twelve months of retroactive entitlement makes it easier for potential beneficiaries to calculate the effect of the retirement test. Instead of having to anticipate earnings, they have information about their actual earnings. Under the law as it pertained to 1977, benefits could clearly be obtained for all months of unemployment after the date of retroactive entitlement and for months in which earnings were below the maximum of $250 allowed by the monthly test.

Even if earnings were high in some of the months following backdated entitlement, the annual earnings test would in many cases have permitted payment for the entire year in which retirement occurred, especially if work stopped fairly early in the calendar year. If the year's earned income exceeded the annual limit, the retroactivity provision was still useful in connection with the annual test. The amount of benefits to be withheld if the annual earnings test were not met was determined by total earnings in a calendar year, regardless of when the worker became entitled to benefits. It was consequently advantageous to have entitlement to a full year's benefits against which to charge the withholding.

A hypothetical illustration, using the 1977 earnings test, demonstrates the combination of retroactive entitlement and annual earnings in excess of $3,000. In the case of a schoolteacher who filed in May 1977 for retroactive entitlement to begin January 1, 1977, her monthly benefit was $250. She taught school from January through May and from September through December 1977 and earned $5,000 for the year.

1. She would receive $250 in retirement benefits for the months of June, July, and August, if she had no other earned income, since she would clearly meet the monthly test.

2. Her annual income is $2,000 in excess of the permitted $3,000.

3. Withholding of $1,000 (half the excess earnings) would occur

---

[8] Carol Zuckert, "Retroactive Entitlement to Benefits," in U.S. Department of Health, Education, and Welfare, Social Security Administration, *Reaching Retirement Age*, Report no. 47 (Washington, D.C., 1976), p. 233.

at a rate of $250 a month beginning in January 1977 and would be completed by the end of April.

4. She would receive $250 for May and for each following month both during the summer vacation and when she was working.

Retroactive entitlement to January 1, 1977, was helpful to this teacher because it gave her the maximum number of months of benefits against which to charge the withholding. This was a basic intention of Congress in allowing up to twelve months of retroactive entitlement. The provision allows some flexibility in choosing an advantageous entitlement date in line with the retirement test and the individual's recent earnings history.

The 1977 amendments to the Social Security Act placed a limit on retroactive benefits in that the initial month of eligibility for such benefits cannot result in a permanently reduced benefit as compared with the amount that would be payable for the month in which the claim is filed. The monthly earnings test is still applicable for the year of retirement in computing retroactive benefits. The new rule curtailing retroactive benefits has reportedly caused more concern among applicants for OASI benefits than any other change made by the 1977 amendments.[9]

Self-Employment

One advantage to the beneficiaries in part-time self-employment after retirement is that they can more readily adjust their efforts to meet the retirement test. They can more easily secure an optimal balance between leisure and total income from work plus social security benefits.

Suppose a man in 1977 owned a large business and earned about $70,000 a year. At age sixty-five he applied for social security benefits but continued to operate the business except that he went abroad during the summer. Since he probably did not render "substantial services" during those months, he would receive his monthly benefits for those months. But his being out of the country during the summer is not necessarily proof that his services are insubstantial. If he were in daily contact with his office, he might not only have a poor vacation but also lose his retirement benefits.

If an American in 1977 were either self-employed abroad or employed by a company that is not covered by the U. S. social security system, the seven-day work test applied. If he worked on any part of

---

[9] According to information received from Sharon Dukes of the Social Security Administration, Tallahassee, Florida, in April 1978.

seven or more days a month, his monthly retirement benefit was withheld, and payments to a spouse or other entitled person were suspended. If he "carried on a trade" abroad as owner or partner, he would be considered to be working on seven or more days a month and would be ineligible for benefits.[10] Presumably it was not considered feasible to check the number of actual days of work under these conditions.

The above examples were based on the law as it existed prior to the 1977 amendments. With elimination of the monthly test, except for the year of retirement, new legal interpretations will have to be made, based only on annual earnings.

If a self-employed person had a net profit above $3,000 in 1977, as reported to the Internal Revenue Service for income tax purposes, the Social Security Administration would usually presume that the one-dollar-in-two penalty for excess annual earnings applied. If, however, the effort had been irregular, the retiree would qualify under the monthly test for all months in which services were not substantial. If net profit from self-employment is low, say, $200 for the year, but the individual had to work more than forty-five hours (or some other determined amount not less than fifteen hours) a month to earn this amount, he would not be entitled to 1977 benefits under the monthly test but could collect full benefits under the annual test.

Some individuals are both self-employed and employed by an outside firm. For purposes of the annual test, net profit from self-employment is added to income from outside employment or a net loss is deducted from total wages reported.[11] If an individual earned $240 as wages in each month of 1977 and also rendered substantial services in self-employment, under the 1977 monthly test he was not entitled to benefits. If his self-employment net income turned out to be only $1,000 his total 1977 income would be $3,880; thus $440 in social security benefits would be withheld, and he could collect the remainder.

Some Further Legal Details

A substantial body of law applying to social security is set forth in the *Social Security Handbook*, in *Social Security Rulings*, and elsewhere. Some of the more interesting provisions related to the retirement test, especially relatively recent rulings, are described here without any claim to completeness.

---

[10] *Social Security Handbook*, pp. 304–05.
[11] Ibid., p. 297.

It is not surprising that some of the social security regulations strongly resemble those of the Internal Revenue Service, especially since income tax information is used as a check on postretirement earnings. But the regulations and definitions are not identical. In a recent ruling a salesman working on a straight commission felt that he could deduct his traveling expenses for purposes of meeting the social security retirement test as he could do for income tax purposes. It was ruled that this deduction could not be made in the social security earnings report. For the year of the ruling, however, he was deemed to be "without fault" since recovery of the benefits would have deprived him of current income required for living expenses.[12]

This illustrates a basic flaw in the retirement test. The deductions permitted for income tax purposes (while sometimes constituting loopholes) have in part evolved to protect the taxpayer. Travel expenses in connection with employment, large medical expenses, alimony payments, and capital losses are a few allowable deductions that can soften life's blows. The retirement test does not take into consideration special needs for additional income based on unfortunate situations or job-related expenses.

The Social Security Administration, unlike the Internal Revenue Service, pays great attention to when income is *earned* rather than when it is paid. An applicant for retirement benefits arranged with her employer to pay her less than the permitted monthly amount but to pay a substantial "Christmas bonus," which brought her monthly average above the permitted amount. The ruling went against her since the bonus was found to be a deferred payment of previous earnings.[13]

An executive who arranged for deferred payment of part of his salary until after retirement—thus reducing total income taxes—fared well in collecting social security retirement benefits. Since the income was *earned* before retirement, even though paid later, it was ruled not to count against him for the earnings test.[14]

The Social Security Administration is concerned about whether income is earned or unearned and about attempts to convert the former into the latter in order to evade the retirement test. "Dividends" from a closely held corporation (which may actually be payment in lieu of salary for services performed by the social security beneficiary) are supposed to be scrutinized carefully.

---

[12] U.S. Department of Health, Education, and Welfare, Social Security Administration, *Social Security Rulings on Federal Old-Age Survivors, Disability, Health Insurance, and Black Lung Benefits* (Washington, D.C., November 1974), p. 35.
[13] *Social Security Rulings*, January 1974, p. 7.
[14] Ibid., July 1973, p. 19.

Income that is not counted for purposes of the annual earnings test includes:

- Pension and retirement pay
- Payments in kind for domestic service, agricultural labor, or for work not done in the course of the employer's trade or business
- Rentals from real estate where the beneficiary did not "materially" participate in work connected with the income
- Interest or dividends on bonds or stocks
- Capital gains
- Tips under $20 per month or not in cash
- Reimbursement of travel expenses
- Payment for moving expenses
- Royalties if the patent was obtained before the age of sixty-five and no substantial improvements were made after that age.

Milton Friedman has pointed out that the U.S. federal income tax is really a broad-based excise tax that inevitably leaves untouched goods and services not produced through the market—leisure, household activities, and most other income in kind.[15] The Social Security Administration's definition of earned income for purposes of the retirement test encounters the same problem with respect to income in kind. If such income does not go through the market it escapes detection, except where it is clearly attached to dollar income as in the case of free housing to an employee. The explicit exemption of some varieties of income in kind suggests that it is probably infeasible to attempt to count many other varieties.

Theorists sometimes consider leisure to be a form of income. Over a span of years American society has chosen to take a growing share of its income in the form of leisure and a decreasing share in the form of goods and services. This practice adds to the inequity of the earnings test. An individual who does not work at all after retirement from his main job is taking his income in the form of leisure without penalty. But an individual who chooses to take his income in the form of traceable wages or salary can encounter the penalty imposed by the social security law.

---

[15] Milton Friedman, "The Welfare Effects of an Income Tax and an Excise Tax," *Essays in Positive Economics* (Chicago: University of Chicago Press, 1953), p. 112.

3
Earned Income versus Property Income

The distinction between earned and unearned income, although basic to the retirement test, has never been clear. According to the classical trinity of factors of production—land, labor, and capital—the distinction appears to be neat, with earned income being only the return to labor. Even in the view of the classical economists, however, the return to capital was sometimes considered to be the reward for "abstinence"—the usually painful conduct of building capital by saving and subsequently of maintaining the capital by refraining from its consumption.

Nassau W. Senior popularized the concept of abstinence, which became one line of criticism of the Marxian labor theory of value.[1] Although the connotation of pain is scarcely appropriate when a large fortune has been inherited (as the socialist writers were quick to point out), individuals who have personally abstained from consumption to build a modest capital usually feel that they have "earned" the interest received. If capital gains are made through price appreciation, the gainer may well feel that he has earned the sum by wise investment, perhaps accompanied by much study of alternatives and consequent sacrifice of leisure and other opportunities.

Human Capital

Development of the concept of human capital in recent years has further blurred the distinction between earned and unearned income. Investment in the individual is now seen to be similar in many ways to investment in material resources. Formal education, vocational training, on-the-job training, and even expenditures on health, on

---

[1] Nassau W. Senior, *Political Economy* (London: Charles Griffen & Co., 1879).

migration, and on searching for information about prices and incomes have been viewed as investments in human capital.[2] The income of a well-educated individual is likely to exceed that of an unskilled worker by a large amount, and most of the difference is best viewed as interest on the additional investment in his person. (Part is probably due to greater ability.) Interest earnings on material and human capital are consequently not inherently unlike. Abstinence is also required in the building of human capital—for example, time spent in study and practice could be spent in other, perhaps more pleasurable, ways. Abstinence is similarly needed to preserve human capital by means of continued study, practice, and diversion of resources to personal health care.

According to Frank H. Knight, there is really only one factor of production—capital.[3] Most of the value of land is derived from investment in clearing, draining, filling, and infrastructure, and most of the productivity of labor is due to investment in the human agent.

For many persons and under many conditions during their lifetimes, material resources and human resources are practical alternatives for investment. Yet interest from following the former course is considered by law to be "unearned income" while equivalent interest derived from the latter course is called "earned income." Definitions are often unimportant, but not when they affect such important government activities as tax collection and the payment of benefits.

An individual who has invested heavily in his own human capital is much more likely to be able to earn substantial income after retirement from his main job than can an individual who has relied largely on untutored labor power.[4] The postretirement possibilities of engineers, doctors, accountants, lawyers, tax experts, and professors and also of such skilled persons as automobile mechanics, electricians, carpenters, truck drivers, and plumbers are obvious. This extra income is largely interest on human capital acquired by education, experience,

---

[2] Gary S. Becker, *Human Capital*, 2d ed. (New York: Columbia University Press, 1975), p. 9.

[3] Frank H. Knight, "The Ricardian Theory of Production and Distribution," in *On the History and Method of Economics: Selected Essays* (Chicago: University of Chicago Press, 1956), p. 57.

[4] According to my calculations, based on four censuses among white males in the South, maximum human capital is attained at about age forty-eight. College graduates and those with postgraduate schooling have about two and a half times as much human capital as those with only eight years of formal schooling. The relative advantage of the former is likely to be even greater at later years. See Marshall R. Colberg, "Age-Human Capital Profiles for Southern Men," *Review of Business and Economic Research*, vol. 11, no. 2 (Winter 1975–1976), p. 70.

on-the-job training, and similar investment. Interest on this form of capital encounters the problem of the social security earnings test while interest on material capital escapes the test.

Earned Income and the Income Tax

The distinction between earned income and other income is less important for income tax purposes than for the social security retirement test. However, the recent introduction of an earned income credit into federal income tax law increases the importance of the definitions. Under current law the earned income tax credit to families with children is 10 percent of the first $4,000 of earned income, providing a maximum credit of $400. This credit is reduced by an amount equal to 10 percent of adjusted gross income in excess of $4,000. If earned income exceeds adjusted gross income the reduction is based instead on the total amount of earned income. This provides a negative tax of as much as $400 on earned income.[5]

For present purposes, an interesting aspect of this relatively new income tax provision is that it favors low-income persons who receive earned income over low-income persons who receive income only from rent, interest, dividends, pensions, and the like. This is just the opposite of the philosophy underlying the social security earnings test, which gives unearned income preferential treatment. The distinction between earned and other income does not stand up well to close examination. If, however, one type is to be favored it should probably be earned income, in part because such income requires current personal exertion, while income from material capital can result from inheritance or from an earlier receipt of gifts. Henry Simons emphasized that gifts received can best be considered as part of current income, although tax law has trained us not to think in this way.[6]

Housewives' Services

Housewives (and even some husbands) provide labor inputs into household productive activity that would be extremely costly if pro-

---

[5] Richard A. Musgrave and Peggy Musgrave, *Public Finance in Theory and Practice* (New York: McGraw-Hill, 1973), "Memorandum to Users," June 1, 1977.
[6] Henry Simons, *Personal Income Taxation* (Chicago: University of Chicago Press, 1938), p. 207. Simons maintains that gifts (except for small ones) should be counted as part of income for tax purposes.

cured in the market.[7] The real income secured by the family from its own household productive activity neither pays taxes to build up postretirement benefits nor counts against the family in the earnings test. Yet the social security law provides that the wife of a retired worker can receive an allowance equal to half her husband's primary insurance amount when she first claims benefits at age sixty-five (or a reduced amount at age sixty-two). If she is entitled to a retirement benefit based on her own earnings record and this is larger, she is entitled only to her own primary insurance amount.

Marilyn Flowers, reasoning in a framework of public choice, feels that with the large increase since 1939 in women's participation in the labor force it is no surprise that the dependent-spouse provisions of the Social Security Act have become increasingly unpopular.[8] Married women with substantial work histories may get little or no more in retirement benefits than women who have worked only in the household. Like the retirement test, this characteristic of the benefit structure tends to reduce labor force participation of older women. Since a recent decision of the U.S. Supreme Court, the Social Security Administration has been ordered by the Court to extend benefits to husbands and widowers of covered women on the same basis as to wives and widows.[9] Labor force participation of older men is probably somewhat reduced by this Supreme Court ruling. For example, a man who has worked solely under the federal civil service retirement program has less incentive to build up OASI credit if his wife has earned a substantial social security retirement benefit.

For the retirement test, the provision of retirement benefits based on the spouse's earnings record increases the advantage of income in kind over dollar income. A housewife (or househusband) can receive substantial benefits based on the spouse's earnings record and can readily meet the retirement test so long as she (or he) does not work for dollar income. The same is true, of course, if the benefits are based on her (or his) own earnings record. Services derived from home

---

[7] Jack Hirshleifer, *Price Theory and Applications* (Englewood Cliffs, N.J.: Prentice-Hall, 1976), p. 381. Hirshleifer points out that although the theorist usually analyzes the choice between income and leisure, the latter does not necessarily mean a mere lazing away of one's time but covers all nonmarket productive activities.

[8] Marilyn R. Flowers, *Women and Social Security: An Institutional Dilemma* (Washington, D.C.: American Enterprise Institute for Public Policy Research, 1977), chap. 3.

[9] Flowers, *Women and Social Security*, p. 27. Divorced husbands, however, are not entitled to benefits on the basis of their former wives' primary insurance amounts. There are also some other differences in the treatment of men and women.

ownership constitute a very important source of income to retired people that escapes the earnings test.

A worker who receives old-age retirement benefits under the social security law usually feels that he has bought the pension through payroll taxes (that have become decidedly stiff in recent years). He is not likely to think in terms of "an intergenerational tax-transfer system" in which his benefits are being paid by younger workers. And he is likely to resent the lack of an earnings limitation in most other retirement plans except for further work under the same plan.

Civil Service Retirement System

The federal civil service retirement program, which predated social security, could have been coordinated with OASI but was kept entirely separate. An expert in the field of pensions, Robert J. Myers, attributes the separation to consistent opposition by federal employee organizations. He points out that career employees can often qualify under both programs and enjoy a substantial advantage. The social security benefit formulas are favorable not only to relatively poor people but also to those who only "look" poor because of low covered earnings during a short period of time.[10] The retirement test under federal civil service requires only retirement from federal employment and permits further work under consultant contracts.

Postal employees, with their strong union, remained with the civil service retirement system when the postal system was converted from a regular government department to an independent corporation. The Tennessee Valley Authority and the Board of Governors of the Federal Reserve System, however, have established plans that include OASDI coverage (that is, OASI plus disability insurance).[11]

Military Pensions

Members of the military forces are covered under OASDI and Medicare as are most workers in the country. Their taxable wages are equivalent to their cash pay. Creditable wages include cash pay plus $100 per month for all ranks as an allowance for income in kind. In addition,

---

[10] Robert J. Myers, *Social Security* (Homewood, Ill.: Richard D. Irwin, Inc., 1975), p. 572. This is probably an important reason that over half the early retirees under civil service take new jobs. See Lenore E. Bixby, "Retirement Patterns in the United States: Research and Policy Interaction," *Social Security Bulletin*, vol. 39 (August 1976), p. 10.

[11] Ibid., pp. 580–81.

there are noncontributory pensions from the federal government, usually after only twenty years of service.[12] Second careers are consequently extremely common among former military personnel. The only earnings test for a military pension applies to regular retired officers who work for the federal government. They are presently required to forfeit half their annual retired pay above $4,219.10 while working for the federal government. Reserve officers and enlisted people are not subject to this penalty, and it is a constant source of complaint by regular officers that they are subjected to discriminatory treatment.

State and Local Plans

A wide variety of state and local retirement systems exist. Teachers and other public employees often have separate plans. Police and firemen usually have their own (more liberal) benefits. Over half of all state and local employees who have a retirement system are also under OASDI.[13] One problem that is unlikely to have been pointed out to employees is that the social security earnings test applies to part of the retirement benefit. Where OASI benefits supplement a state pension to bring the total pension to the amount previously furnished by the state alone, the social security retirement test may make the package plan less desirable by penalizing the retiree for extra income.

Private Plans

Over 42 million persons are reported to be covered by major private pension plans in the United States.[14] Only social security coverage is larger. There is almost complete duplication in coverage, of course.

Among the strongly unionized electrical, automobile, and steel workers, for example, generous "thirty and out" plans have gained popularity.[15] Alfred Skolnik reported that the increase in early retirement provisions has been most striking among multiemployer plans.[16] The proportion of employees covered by early retirement provisions in such plans rose from 23 percent in 1960 to 82 percent in 1973. The shift downward to age fifty-five was found to be continuing.

---

[12] Ibid., p. 590.
[13] Ibid., p. 588.
[14] American Council of Life Insurance, *Pension Facts 1976* (New York, 1976).
[15] Jerry Flint, "Early Retirement Is Growing in U.S.," *New York Times*, July 10, 1977, p. 1.
[16] Alfred M. Skolnik, "Private Pension Plans, 1950–74," *Social Security Bulletin*, vol. 39 (June 1976), pp. 3–17.

A large number of private plans supplement the OASI early retirement benefit with a special payment to age sixty-five or the age when reduced OASI benefits begin. These plans often permit the worker to receive a level income throughout retirement—initially from the private pension alone and then from the combined pension and social security.

Only a small percentage of private plans have been adequately indexed to forestall the inroads of inflation. In a great many cases early beneficiaries of private retirement plans earn supplementary income. They may be largely unaware of the social security earned income test until benefits under that program begin. They then find that the earnings test makes it difficult to maintain the real income level enjoyed before private pension benefits were partially replaced by social security. As mentioned earlier, this is also a problem in the common combination of state and local retirement benefits and social security.

4
Recommendations by the Quadrennial Advisory Council on Social Security and Others

The social security earnings test has spawned a huge volume of letters of complaint to newspaper and magazine editors, to congressmen, and to the Social Security Administration. These letters often point out that when income and social security payroll taxes and the 50 percent penalty for excess earnings are considered, the combined effect is to make many recipients of social security old-age benefits (under age seventy-two) the most heavily taxed segment of the population.[1]

Congressmen regularly introduce a great number of bills to amend the Social Security Act and often include provisions to liberalize or eliminate the earnings test.[2] The most frequent provision is to eliminate the retirement test at age sixty-five. Proposed increases in the amount of unpenalized annual earnings are also common.

The Position of the Social Security Administration

The Social Security Administration has consistently favored retention of an earnings test although it has often recommended liberalization as inflation has squeezed the real value of earnings. In its 1962 *Annual Report*, the Department of Health, Education, and Welfare stated with unusual clarity: "An ideal retirement test would be one that would not deter any retired person from seeking an opportunity to do all the

---

[1] A recent example is a letter from Carl L. Roberts, aged sixty-seven, published in the *Congressional Record*, vol. 123 (June 9, 1977), p. S9357, in which he calculates a tax rate of 73.1 percent on his vacation pay of $816.92.

[2] As of February 6, 1976, a total of 1,629 bills to reform the social security laws had been introduced into the House of Representatives since the session began in January. See *President's Social Security Proposals*, Public Hearings before the Subcommittee on Social Security, Committee on Ways and Means, House of Representatives, 94th Congress, 2d session (Washington, D.C., 1976), testimony of Fernand J. St Germain, representative from Rhode Island, p. 449.

work he wants, but would also prevent payment of benefits to people who are working full time. Unfortunately no test will accomplish this."[3]

A preference for "social adequacy" over individual equity has governed the official position with respect to the work-income test. The Social Security Administration's position is that old-age insurance benefits are not intended as an annuity to be paid merely because an individual reaches a certain age; instead they are intended to assure a regular income after retirement. As pointed out in Chapter 1, Paul H. Douglas immediately detected the confusion between relief and insurance in the Social Security Act and predicted the constant problems that this would create. Advocates of a retirement test are emphasizing a presumptive need for relief as the more important criterion. The test is very crude, however, since it omits all measurement of unearned income, other pensions, assets, number of dependents, and so on. The Social Security Administration emphasizes that to pay annuities to fully employed persons past age sixty-five (or sixty-two) but under seventy-two would be costly, using up money that can better go to poorer families. Further, it is argued by proponents of the test that persons of low income-earning ability can receive partial or even full social security retirement benefits while continuing to work since they will not be hit hard by the earnings test.

Wallis Advisory Council Recommendation

The 1975 Advisory Council on Social Security, chaired by Allen W. Wallis, agreed basically with the Social Security Administration that the retirement test is consistent with the purpose of the program. The most frequently discussed alternative—payment to all eligible persons at age sixty-five—was considered to be "too expensive." The Advisory Council admitted, however, that the present test may permit little extra income if income and OASDHI (that is, with hospital insurance too) payroll taxes, state and local taxes, and work-related expenses are considered.[4] The report recommended different treatment for three levels of earned income:

1. There should be no withholding of benefits for income up to $2,520 per year.

---

[3] U.S. Department of Health, Education, and Welfare, *Annual Report, 1962* (Washington, D.C., 1962), p. 35.
[4] *Reports of the Quadrennial Advisory Council on Social Security*, House Document no. 94-75, 94th Congress, 1st session (Washington, D.C., March 1975), pp. 199-201.

2. One dollar in three should be withheld for earnings between $2,520 and $5,040.

3. One dollar in two should be withheld for earned income above $5,040 per year.

For 1977 the equivalent would have been no withholding up to $3,000, one dollar in three for earnings between $3,000 and $6,000, and one dollar in two for earnings above $6,000. Munnell states that this liberalization would cost about $670 million at 1977 levels.[5] Whatever one thinks of the Advisory Council's recommendation, reinstituting a three-level earnings test, which was abandoned in 1973, would further complicate the already difficult problem of administering the test.

The 1975 Advisory Council also recommended that the monthly test be eliminated except for the year in which retirement occurs. An advantage would be simplification of administration. Self-employed persons would be put more nearly on the same basis as those who work for wages, and for those with both kinds of income, the dollar sum of earned income, as defined for income tax purposes, could be used. There would still be some relative advantage in being self-employed since control over the accounting makes it more feasible to shift net income between years, and alternative depreciation formulas and other devices can be used to keep net income within bounds in a particular year.

Some unusual situations created by the monthly test as it existed prior to 1978 were pointed out in Chapter 2. Rita Ricardo Campbell cites the possibility that eligible persons on a company board of directors may receive an annual lump sum payment exceeding the annual exempt amount and still collect benefits in each of the other eleven months.[6] It is easy, however, to exaggerate the importance of such unusual cases. Retention of the monthly test is an aid to retired persons who are able to work a great deal during some months but not in others, especially when employment is highly dependent on the inflow of orders. An annual test alone would tend to reduce retirement benefits by a greater amount and thereby reduce the availability of partly retired persons for irregular work activity.

---

[5] Alicia H. Munnell, "Social Security," *New England Economic Review* (Federal Reserve Bank of Boston, July/August 1977), p. 42.

[6] This would be true only if meetings were held in only one month, since time of earning rather than time of payment is considered by the Social Security Administration. Rita Ricardo Campbell, "The Problems of Fairness," in Michael J. Boskin, ed., *The Crisis in Social Security* (San Francisco: Institute for Contemporary Studies, 1977), p. 142.

Hsaio Committee Recommendation

The Consultant Panel on Social Security, with William C. L. Hsaio, a former deputy chief actuary of the Social Security Administration, as chairman, recommended in 1976 that the retirement test be retained.

As long as replacing income lost as a result of retirement, death, or disability is an important goal of the System, some methods for defining income loss must exist. A major liberalization or elimination of the test is not consistent with the goals of the System as developed over the past forty years. The elimination of the retirement test would, by current standards, produce "windfall" benefits.[7]

But the goals of the system have never been clear. In the early years the goal of relief necessarily predominated since needy families had not yet made sufficient contributions for any sort of annuity to be paid. With over four decades of payroll tax collections, the system is now mature enough for a sharp swing in the direction of individual equity, with pensions related fairly closely to individual payments over a substantial period. As stated by James M. Buchanan, "One of the chief sources of crisis in the existing social security system is the observed tendency of politicians, especially in recent years, to confuse the achievement of social insurance objectives with the relief of primary and secondary poverty and to load the same set of institutions with these quite different burdens."[8]

It is beyond the scope of the present study to suggest an entirely new structure in which social insurance and relief are adequately separated, perhaps financed by entirely different sets of taxes. Instead, the retirement test is viewed as one provision of the present system that can be changed (as it was in the 1977 amendments) and is open to further change.

The appeal by the Consultant Panel on Social Security to the alleged goals of the system is not a convincing argument for retaining the retirement test. But the immediate windfalls to persons still fully employed beyond possible retirement age does raise serious questions of both equity and cost to the system. If the social security system had not moved partly away from the insurance principle in the early years, annuities from the federal government at a specified age would

---

[7] *A Plan for Rebuilding Social Security*, Preliminary Report of the Consultant Panel on Social Security, February 1976, pp. 4–14.

[8] James M. Buchanan, "Social Insurance in a Growing Economy: A Proposal for Radical Reform," *National Tax Journal*, vol. 21 (December 1968), p. 388.

have been a natural expectation. An alleged windfall would result now only because of the change in expectations owing to the way in which the social security law has evolved. Still, the cost problem may make a *gradual* change in the work-income test more feasible than immediate elimination of the test. When viewed in real terms, however, the change in the retirement test effected by the 1977 legislation is far *too* gradual.

Myers's Position on the Test

The chief actuary of the Social Security Administration from 1947 to 1970, Robert J. Myers, favors retention of the retirement test in his comprehensive book, *Social Security*. He makes the following point:

> It would seem that many aged persons who cannot be gainfully employed use the earnings test as perhaps an unnecessary alibi to explain their not working. Moreover, if some people need substantial earnings to supplement their OASDI benefits to live on, then it would seem that the entire benefit level is too low for the vast majority who cannot work.

Myers's "alibi" idea seems to be without great merit. To whom does the retiree have to provide an alibi—a spouse, the social security office, the Internal Revenue Service? The suggestion that the entire benefit level is too low is undoubtedly true when OASI constitutes most or all of the income. But Myers appears to understate the actual and potential labor force participation of older persons when he goes on to say, "Countering this is the fact that only about ten percent of those over age sixty-five have any significant earnings at all, and many of these earn far less than the maximum possible for full receipt of benefits."[9] A more recent study by the Social Security Administration states that 44.6 percent of men aged sixty-five to sixty-nine had work experience while 22.5 percent of men above seventy had such experience.[10] Over three-fourths of the men and over two-fifths of the women, aged sixty-two to sixty-four, had work experience in each of the past few years.

In terms of the better-known labor force participation rate, which pertains to an average week of the year, Colin and Rosemary Campbell note a drop among men aged sixty-five and over from 48 percent

---

[9] Robert J. Myers, *Social Security* (Homewood, Ill.: Richard D. Irwin, Inc., 1975), p. 185.

[10] Lenore E. Bixby, "Retirement Patterns in the United States: Research and Policy Interaction," *Social Security Bulletin*, vol. 39 (August 1976), pp. 3–19.

in 1947 to 22 percent in 1974.[11] The rate for men aged sixty-five to sixty-nine in 1974 is considerably higher, 32.9 percent. (And as noted above it is still higher when measured by the number who engage at any time of the year in gainful employment.) If do-it-yourself activities were counted, the percentage who work would be very high.

A critical factor in the question of altering the social security retirement test is the effect this would have on work for pay by the elderly. Michael J. Boskin, basing his research on a national sample of 5,000 households in the Panel Study of Income Dynamics, feels that "liberalization of the earnings test would dramatically reduce the probability of retirement and improve the allocation of resources."[12] Boskin calculates that "a reduction in the implicit tax on earnings from one half to one third cuts the annual probability of retirement in half for typical workers." If reasonably accurate, this suggests that the recommendation by the Advisory Council on Social Security with respect to the excess earnings penalty would markedly increase labor force participation by OASI recipients. (Abolition of the test would be even more effective.)

Peter A. Diamond, a member of the Consultant Panel on Social Security, has advocated an experiment, along lines used to experiment with effects of a negative income tax, to see how people would actually react to a change in the earnings limitation.[13]

Other Recommendations Regarding the Test

Among outside scholars who have recently studied the U.S. social security system, there is a good deal of support for eliminating or liberalizing the earnings test. Kip Viscusi and Richard Zeckhauser recommend removal of the earnings test for social security as the "first priority." Although they say that benefit costs would increase with such a change, "sources of revenue do exist to finance such a change." They also suggest that the income taxes of the working elderly be earmarked for social security to preserve the image of the program and the dignity of recipients.[14] This would require a move in the direction of general revenue financing of OASDHI benefits.

---

[11] Colin D. Campbell and Rosemary G. Campbell, "Conflicting Views on the Effect of Old-Age and Survivors' Insurance on Retirement," *Economic Inquiry*, vol. 14 (September 1976), p. 370.

[12] Michael J. Boskin, "Social Security and Retirement Decisions," *Economic Inquiry*, vol. 15 (January 1977), pp. 13–20.

[13] *President's Social Security Proposals*, testimony of Peter A. Diamond, p. 407.

[14] W. Kip Viscusi and Richard Zeckhauser, "The Role of Social Security in Income Maintenance," in Boskin, ed., *The Crisis in Social Security*, p. 63.

Munnell appears to be cautiously favorable to liberalization of the retirement test:

> In sum, there is a good reason to be concerned about the provision of the social security law that discourages labor force participation of people over sixty-two who prefer to continue working. By limiting available income sources, such a deterrent reduces the welfare of the elderly. The burden falls particularly heavily on low-income people, who seldom have other sources of retirement income such as private insurance, pension benefits, or savings. In addition, any provision that encourages a smaller labor force in future years will force a significantly higher tax rate in the long run.[15]

At a two-day conference on social security held at the Brookings Institution in 1976, a main topic was whether the social adequacy function of social security should be reduced or transferred to the supplemental security income program (ssi). With respect to the work-income test, it was reported:

> Many of the participants favored liberalizing the earnings test, although they found it impossible to agree on a specific suggestion given the lack of information on how much the earnings test affects the labor supply. If the effect is significant, it might be worth $2 billion to $3 billion a year to eliminate the test completely at sixty-five. There was little support for eliminating it at sixty-two because it would encourage workers to elect permanently reduced benefits while continuing to work. In addition, it would be very expensive, costing between $6 billion and $7 billion annually.[16]

Raising the Retirement Age

An alternative way to increase labor force participation among older persons is to raise the age at which social security benefits may be secured. In a system financed on a pay-as-you-go basis, the trend toward early retirement is said to place an increasing strain on younger workers to support retired persons. (This view is quite different from the depression-induced view that early retirement frees jobs for younger people.)

It would be extremely disruptive to present-day Americans to raise the ages of eligibility for social security benefits suddenly. Con-

---

[15] Alicia H. Munnell, *The Future of Social Security* (Washington, D.C.: The Brookings Institution, 1977), p. 82.
[16] Ibid., p. 152.

sequently the 1975 Advisory Council on Social Security suggested that a feasible plan would increase the retirement age by one month every six months beginning in 2005 and ending in 2023. By the latter year, the regular retirement age would have increased to sixty-eight and the early retirement age to sixty-five.[17] This proposal seems conducive to a gradual change in personal expectations, private pension plans, and other related matters. The regular retirement age would become sixty-six in 2011 and sixty-seven in 2017.

Delayed Retirement Credit

Another way to encourage later retirement is to increase the delayed retirement credit. Prior to the 1977 amendments benefits were increased by only 1 percent for each year that a worker received no benefits between ages sixty-five and seventy-two. (If a worker received benefits for two vacation months, for example, his eventual full benefit rose by five-sixths of 1 percent for that year's work activity.) The new law increases the incremental rate to 3 percent, but only for those attaining age sixty-two after 1978. The same percentage increase is applicable to widows' and widowers' benefits.

The small (1 or 3 percent) increment to retirement benefits is inconsistent with the recently approved federal law which for most workers prohibits mandatory retirement before age seventy. The retirement test would be less objectionable if an actuarially determined equivalent of about 8 percent per year were added for each year retirement was deferred between ages sixty-two and seventy.[18] If an increment of this dimension were available, the individual would be given a fairer choice among alternative retirement ages between sixty-two and seventy. Individual choice would depend on such matters as health, agreeableness of occupation, income prospects, and average mortality prospects (which vary ethnically).

In Norway, workers who defer retirement beyond age sixty-seven receive a 9 percent increment a year for each year to age seventy. Since 1971 a number of countries including the Central African Republic, El Salvador, the Federal Republic of Germany, Malta, Panama (and the United States since 1972) have initiated pecuniary incentives for work beyond the usual retirement age.[19] As noted, the incentive is small in the United States.

---

[17] *Reports of the Quadrennial Advisory Council on Social Security*, p. 117.

[18] Suggested in private correspondence by Robert J. Myers.

[19] Martin B. Tracy, "World Developments and Trends in Social Security," *Social Security Bulletin*, vol. 39 (April 1976), p. 19.

In general, the provision of a substantial economic incentive to delayed retirement seems preferable to raising the normal age of eligibility for OASI benefits above sixty-five. Even if the age increase were gradual and effective only in the next century, workers would be apt to feel cheated by such a change in the law. Many persons will note only the higher retirement age requirements in newspaper accounts and will be unduly alarmed, not realizing that the effective date is far off. Fuller congressional consideration of the delayed retirement credit is desirable. The limited liberalization provided by the 1977 amendments was apparently designed rather hastily "to strengthen work incentives under the decoupled system."[20] Greater liberalization would be compatible with the federal goal of later retirement of able-bodied Americans.

Retirement Test in Other Countries

Retirement tests have been a cause of great public and governmental concern in the social security systems of other countries as well as the United States. Juanita Kreps examined fifty-seven retirement plans in different countries, of which thirty-seven had some sort of retirement condition and twenty had no retirement test. She concluded that "With only one exception, the twenty schemes having no retirement test were content with their arrangements, whereas about half of the thirty-seven having such tests reported some sentiment for changing the regulations."[21] It is possible, however, that the meaning of "retirement test" is not uniform in all countries and plans examined by Kreps.

The Social Security Administration has reported: "The extent of withdrawal from the labor force that is required for receipt of a pension in many countries continues to lessen."[22] This provision has been eliminated altogether in Canada, Ghana, and Singapore since 1973. The Federal Republic of Germany is among the larger countries without an earnings test, except in the case of early retirement. At the other extreme, the U.S.S.R. has a complicated test in which pensions are suspended if concurrent earnings exceed 100 rubles per month, but there is no reduction if the earnings are in mining, industrial

---

[20] U.S. Department of Health, Education, and Welfare, Social Security Administration, *Social Security Rulings on Federal Old-Age Survivors, Disability, Health Insurance, and Black Lung Benefits* (Washington, D.C., January 1978), p. 29.

[21] Juanita M. Kreps, *Lifetime Allocation of Work and Income* (Durham, N.C.: Duke University Press, 1971), p. 72.

[22] U.S. Department of Health, Education, and Welfare, Social Security Administration, *Social Security Programs Throughout the World, 1975*, Research Report no. 48 (Washington, D.C., December 1975), p. xii.

labor, or certain service industries and only a partial reduction for some other occupations and for certain geographical locations.[23] A test of this complexity, however, is bound to generate innumerable interpersonal inequities and much dissatisfaction.

Recommendation of Committee for Economic Development

A January 1978 publication of the Committee for Economic Development (CED) discusses the social security retirement test briefly. The net cost to the social security system is stated by CED to be "perhaps $2 to $3 billion a year." It is stated that the cost to the federal tax system as a whole might be less than this amount because social security recipients who otherwise would not have worked beyond age sixty-five will pay added income taxes.

The CED recommends that "consideration be given to raising the ceiling on earnings by social security recipients in cases where such earnings are derived from work in which certified labor shortages exist."[24] In my opinion this suggestion would move the United States in the direction already taken by the U.S.S.R. of incorporating in the earnings test detailed bureaucratic determination of the social usefulness of different types of work. More harm than good is likely to result from the interplay of forces generated by special interest groups, and the inherent difficulty of the statistical process of finding where "labor shortages" exist. A further objection is that the already difficult problem of administering the earnings test would be substantially increased.

---

[23] Ibid., p. 232.
[24] Research and Policy Committee for Economic Development, *Jobs for the Hard-to-Employ* (New York: Committee for Economic Development, January 1978), p. 51.

5
Cost of Eliminating the Test

The preceding chapters have shown substantial support for elimination or further liberalization of the social security retirement test. The main problem cited by the Social Security Administration and others is the added cost to the system at a time when the relation of future revenues and costs is a matter of widespread concern. Persons past retirement age, but ineligible for benefits because of their large earnings, would receive a substantial windfall if the test were repealed. Persons receiving reduced benefits because of the test would add more moderately to the cost of the system.

Real National Income

Economic truth often can be best inferred by looking at the "real" situation rather than at dollars. Repeal of the earnings test would result in an improved allocation of resources since the work-leisure choice of many older Americans is now distorted by the large implicit tax on their earned income. Unless increased employment of older persons were entirely at the expense of jobs for younger workers, there would be an increase in real national income. There would clearly *not* be a full job-for-job offset since the occupational skills of the oldest and youngest groups are usually different. The lower the skill level, however, the greater the possibility of substitution tends to be. Even close substitutibility might not bring a reduction in employment opportunities for the young, since the whole level of the economy would be raised by greater labor force participation by the elderly.

Cost Estimates for the System

Estimates of the added cost to the system of eliminating the retirement test at age sixty-five usually run between $2 billion and $4 billion per year.[1] Barbara Lingg reported that in 1971 1.3 million persons aged sixty-five through seventy-one had $2.04 billion in benefits withheld because of the earnings test.[2] The amount would undoubtedly be larger if measured in 1977. A recent figure of $3 billion as an upper limit is estimated by Munnell.[3]

As already mentioned, real national income would rise rather than decline with elimination of the work-income test. Viewed in a sufficiently broad context, there should also be dollar saving rather than cost. Full reconciliation of dollar and real accounts is difficult. State and local tax revenues would be increased, and there would be a downward pressure on prices of some goods and services that increased in supply. At the more obvious federal level, several factors stand out:

1. Added income tax collections would accrue from additional earned dollar income as a result of expansion of labor force participation of OASI recipients.

2. Additional payroll tax collections would be made from the added employees and their employers, and from self-employed recipients of old-age benefits.

3. More federal excise taxes would be collected.

4. Underreporting of earned income to the Internal Revenue Service should decline. Since there is cross-reference between annual reports to the Social Security Administration and annual income tax returns, the present stiff penalty for excess earned income gives a special incentive to recipients of old-age benefits to understate income for income tax purposes whenever it is not explicitly reported in full (as by an employer who withholds taxes).[4] This may be an important source of additional federal revenue that would not be picked up even in a sophisticated statistical study of labor force participation or in an

---

[1] The lower figure is given by Robert S. Kaplan and Arnold R. Weber in a paper entitled "A Proposal to Eliminate the Social Security Retirement Test" (Pittsburgh: Graduate School of Industrial Administration, Carnegie-Mellon University, September 1974), p. 4. The higher figure was cited by Senator Barry Goldwater in his article "This Law Robs Our Senior Citizens," *Readers' Digest*, vol. 105 (August 1974), p. 156.

[2] Barbara A. Lingg, "Retired-Worker Beneficiaries Affected by the Annual Earnings Test in 1971," *Social Security Bulletin*, vol. 38 (August 1975), p. 26.

[3] Alicia H. Munnell, "Social Security," *New England Economic Review*, Federal Reserve Bank of Boston (July/August 1977), p. 43.

[4] Somewhat similarly, violations of minimum wage regulations have been common; see George Macesich and Charles T. Stewart, Jr., "Recent Department of Labor Studies of Minimum Wage Effects," *Southern Economic Journal*, vol. 26 (April 1960), pp. 281–90.

actual experiment such as that done in connection with the negative income tax proposal.

5. A decline in Social Security Administration costs would occur since the earnings test is hard to administer. Large numbers of OASI recipients reside in foreign nations where it is difficult or impossible to determine the extent of employment, and especially self-employment, that actually occurs.

Labor Supply in Theory

The discussion above has assumed that OASI beneficiaries would respond to the removal of the earnings test by increasing their labor force participation, namely, that there is a positive slope to the curve relating the net wage rate to work effort. The famous "backbending supply curve" for labor derives from two opposing effects: a higher wage rate makes leisure more expensive so that less is desired and more work effort is forthcoming; but as income goes up, more leisure is desired. At some wage rate the latter effect may dominate the former, causing a backbend in the labor supply curve.

Eligible persons who now hold down their work effort because of the high implicit tax on earned income are not likely to want to buy more leisure with extra net income. According to the Social Security Administration's *Retirement History Study*, 58 percent of the married men, 57 percent of the unmarried men, and 74 percent of the women who intended to retire expected no retirement income other than social security.[5] It seems obvious that a typical recipient of OASI would be anxious to earn more income to meet living expenses if he or she did not encounter the work-income test.

Of the additional tax revenues that would be collected by the federal government, the payroll and income tax collections would be largest. The amount depends on how much labor force participation would increase among those entitled to old-age benefits and on how much they would earn.

Labor Force Participation

Table 5 shows information from the Bureau of the Census on labor force participation by age in 1970. Labor force participation drops sharply at ages sixty-two and sixty-three and at sixty-five and sixty-six

---

[5] Lola M. Irelan, "Retirement History Study: Introduction," in U.S. Department of Health, Education, and Welfare, Social Security Administration, *Almost 65: Baseline Data from the Retirement History Study*, Research Report no. 49 (Washington, D.C., 1976), p. 6.

TABLE 5

POPULATION AND LABOR FORCE PARTICIPATION, 1970 CENSUS

	Men		Women	
Age	Population	Percent in labor force	Population	Percent in labor force
60	903,894	81.3	1,001,518	42.9
61	833,288	79.2	939,703	40.2
62	815,483	72.7	920,600	35.9
63	761,166	67.5	869,416	32.6
64	744,677	63.1	867,886	29.3
65	695,794	47.1	847,372	22.0
66	656,927	41.9	798,040	18.8
67	628,611	38.6	784,092	17.0
68	555,189	35.4	699,412	14.7
69	579,827	31.5	768,448	12.9
70	534,876	26.9	707,658	11.1
71	484,029	24.6	650,823	9.8
72	453,941	22.1	604,826	9.1
73	434,139	19.8	582,295	7.8
74	417,342	17.4	570,135	7.1

SOURCE: U.S. Department of Commerce, Bureau of the Census, *1970 Census of Population, Subject Reports, Employment Status and Work Experience*, Pc(2)-6A, issued April 1, 1973, pp. 31–32.

for both men and women. Since the reference week to which the data apply is often the last week in March, many who would be sixty-five during the year would not yet be that old. The full effect of sixty-five as a common age for retirement consequently is not reflected until age sixty-six.

Exemption from the social security retirement test occurred at seventy-two at the time of the 1970 census. Any stimulation of labor force participation by termination of the work-income test could be expected to show up best at age seventy-three because of the March reference week. To measure this effect, a straight line was fitted (by least squares) to the labor force participation rates for ages sixty-five through seventy-three. As expected, the actual participation at age seventy-three was above the trend line thus calculated, that is, there was a stimulus to work activity when the negative effect of aging (such as declining health and reluctance of employers to hire) is removed. (The least-squares calculations and related data are shown in the appendix.)

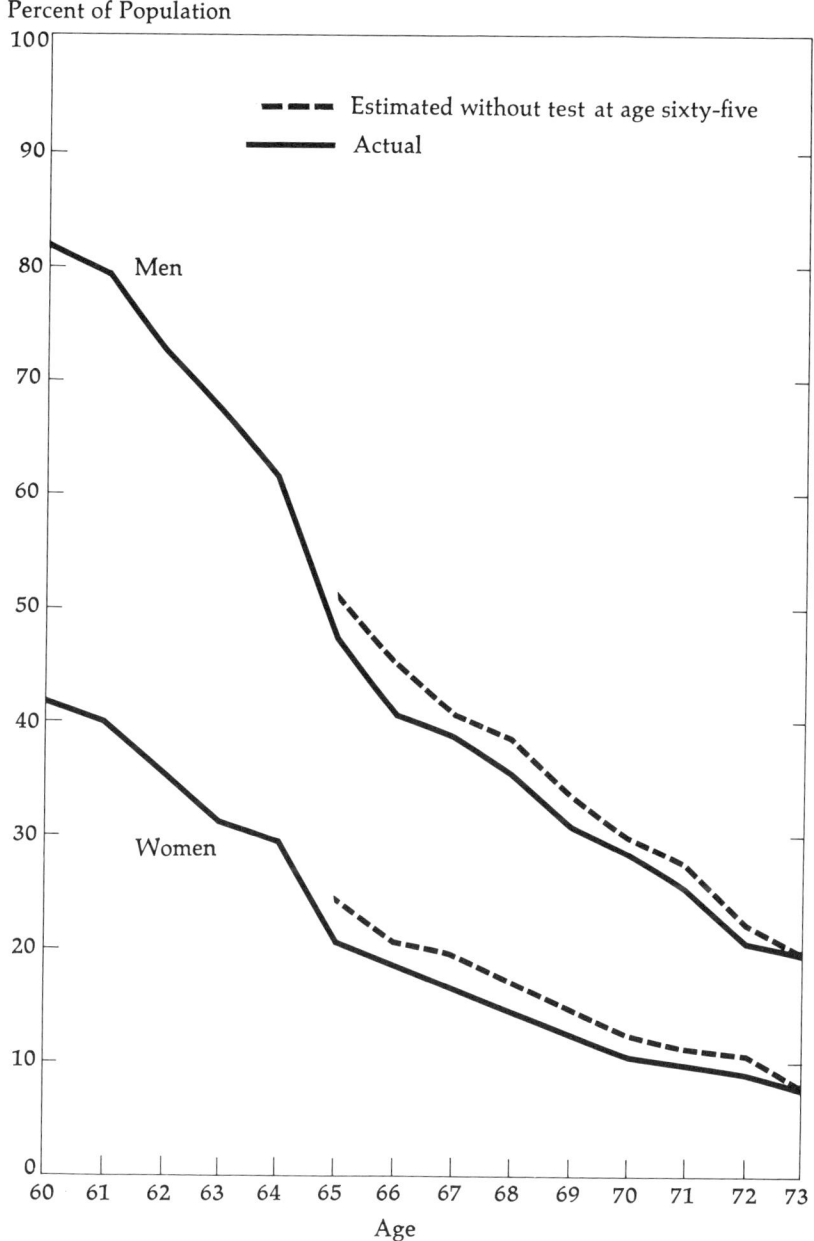

FIGURE 1
LABOR FORCE PARTICIPATION RATES

SOURCE: Table 5 of Chapter 4 and Table 7 of Appendix.

For men, the actual labor force participation rate at age seventy-three was 108 percent of the calculated rate; for women it was 113 percent. These percentages are used to "blow up" actual participation rates for ages sixty-five through seventy-two, the assumption being that with no retirement test the percentage increase in the rate would have been the same as that observed at age seventy-three. Figure 1 shows the actual labor force participation rates for men and women as they were reported in the 1970 census and the higher rates estimated for ages sixty-five through seventy-two on the assumption of no retirement test.

The estimates are admittedly rough. They are, however, based on observed behavior at age seventy-three, and the general appearance of Figure 1 seems plausible since a sharp drop in labor force participation at age sixty-five remains even without the earnings test, owing to other pension plans, union rules, custom, and so on. The estimated line on the chart also shows an incremental participation rate that declines each year after sixty-five, as would probably occur with declining health, negative employer attitudes, and decreased desire to develop new job skills.

Estimated Added Tax Collections

According to estimates shown in the appendix, about $454 million per year would be collected by the federal government in additional payroll and income taxes if the social security earnings test were eliminated at age sixty-five. There is now a double incentive for evasion of some income taxes by persons subject to the retirement test, since honest reporting may also diminish social security benefits. In view of this situation a total of about half a billion dollars per year can conservatively be estimated as additional tax receipts by the federal government in the form of income and payroll levies. Over and above this amount would be the augmented excise and sales tax collections by the federal government and by state and local governments, extra state and local income tax collections, and some other income to government such as license fees, import duties, and the like.

6
Summary

The social security retirement test has always caused great public and governmental concern and will continue to do so until it is eliminated or made innocuous. No issue connected with social security has been the subject of more legislative attempts at amendment, because of the law's uneasy mixture of offering both relief for the needy and annuities, which workers feel they have purchased through payroll deductions over the years.

A freqently introduced amendment has provided for elimination of the earnings test at age sixty-five, in keeping with the annuity view of OASI benefits. The House bill before the 95th Congress in late 1977 contained this provision, effective in 1982, but the final law followed the Senate's approach. In a rather euphemistically labeled section, "Liberalization of Earnings Test for Individuals Age 65 and Over," the 1977 amendments to the Social Security Act delete the (socially useful) monthly earnings test, except for the first year of retirement. Increases in the yearly test are likely to be substantial in real terms only for 1978, with most of the liberalization subsequently scheduled through 1982 a "money illusion." Younger beneficiaries will suffer from the new earnings test, because they will lose the monthly test (except for the first year of retirement) and are allowed to earn only $3,240 without penalty in 1978, with automatic adjustment thereafter.

In real terms the test is substantially more stringent in such cities as Boston, New York, Honolulu, and Anchorage than in most other cities and in rural areas. To adjust the test for cost-of-living differences would, however, unleash a host of political and statistical difficulties.

Unlike the federal income tax law, the law pertaining to the earnings test has no provisions to soften the blow of traveling and other expenses related to work, lack of other income, medical bills, casualty losses, alimony costs, or other particularly unfavorable events of the year.

The test is often more favorable to those residing abroad, since it is much more difficult to check on the amount of work actually performed by these OASI recipients.

The "earned income" concept is nebulous although it is at the heart of the test. Income in kind escapes the test. More important, interest on human capital is treated as earned income while most interest on material capital is considered to be unearned and escapes the test. An exception is some material capital connected with self-employment, since interest on such capital enters into reported net income of the self-employed. If any preference is given it should go to earned income rather than unearned income, which may involve no current personal effort. This anomaly is especially striking in the case of pure rental income on an apartment building, which does not subject an OASI recipient to a penalty, but if he or she has to work in connection with maintenance or rent collection, for example, some or all OASI benefits may be lost. The federal income tax law has recently moved in the opposite direction of *favoring* earned income for low-income families with children.

The special penalty imposed on recipients of OASI benefits is discriminatory when compared with most other retirement plans. Federal civil service retirees, former post office workers, retired military personnel (except for regular officers who take federal jobs), most recipients of private pensions, and many state and local workers who take other employment are not subjected to an earnings test.

Increasingly, OASI benefits are being made a part of private, state, and local pension plans. The earnings test can constitute an unwelcome (and often unexpected) component of plans that were without such qualification prior to the incorporation of social security.

Much of the paperwork faced by OASI recipients is related to the retirement test. Elimination of this extra work would be a boon to many elderly persons and would also speed up the work of local social security offices.

The earnings test would be less objectionable to many people if an actuarially determined increment (say 8 percent) were provided in OASI benefits for each year of delayed retirement. This sort of legislative action seems to be consistent with the new federal law prohibiting (for most persons) mandatory retirement prior to age seventy. While earlier retirement options should continue, persons who delay retirement beyond sixty-five run a considerable risk of not collecting OASI benefits at all. A larger credit for delayed retirement could eliminate this inequity.

The social security earnings test should be eliminated at age sixty-five, possibly on a deferred basis, as in the 1977 House bill, in order to reduce the cost of the system. Until the test is eliminated, the socially useful monthly test should be restored.

The Social Security Retirement Test: Right or Wrong? Wrong!

APPENDIX

To estimate the additional labor force participation that would occur if the earnings test were eliminated at age sixty-five, a straight line was fitted by least squares to the 1970 participation rates for men and women, for ages sixty-five through seventy-three. Any positive deviation from this line at age seventy-three would probably be due to termination of the penalty for excess earnings. The ratio of actual to expected participation at age seventy-three was applied to observed rates at ages sixty-five through seventy-two to secure hypothetical participation rates at these ages. Estimated added participation was calculated by applying these somewhat higher hypothetical participation rates to the July 1, 1976, population estimates of the Census Bureau.

It is difficult to estimate the annual earnings that the hypothetical new labor force participants would have. Presumably they would be lower on average than those already participating in work for wages or salaries or in self-employment, because the more highly paid persons disregard the earnings test in making their employment decisions.

Men aged sixty-five and over who worked full time in the civilian labor force in 1975 had a median income of $11,485, while similarly situated women earned $7,273, according to the *1976 Statistical Abstract of the United States*. Rather arbitrarily, $9,000 was selected as mean earnings of the "new" working males at age sixty-five and $7,000 as mean earnings of the hypothetical new female workers at age sixty-five. In both cases, these earnings were assumed to decline by $250 a year on a straight-line basis by age seventy-three.

Using the equation $Y = a + bX$, with Y being the labor force participation rate and X the age ($X = 1$ for 65, $X = 2$ for 66, and so on), a being the Y intercept, and b the slope, the following equations were derived by least squares:

For men: $Y = 48.9 - 3.4X$
For women: $Y = 22.2 - 1.7X$

From these equations, calculated labor force participation rates were derived. (For example, at age sixty-six for men, the calculated rate Y is equal to $48.9 - 2(3.4)$ or 42.1 percent of the population of that age.) Calculated and actual (1970) participation rates are shown in Table 6. For both men and women, the actual labor force participation exceeded the calculated rate at age seventy-two, and especially at seventy-three, when a full year of exemption from the earnings test was available. For men the actual labor force participation rate at age seventy-three was 108 percent of the calculated rate, while for women the ratio was 113 percent. These percentages were used to "blow up" actual participation rates for ages sixty-five through seventy-two. Added labor force participation rates are shown in Table 7. These are applied to the July 1, 1976, population estimates to calculate the number of additional men and women who would have been working at each age if there had been no earnings test.

Table 8 shows the estimated additional wage and salary and self-employment incomes that the added male workers would generate. The former are multiplied by the 1977 combined employee-employer payroll tax rate of 11.7 percent and the latter by the self-employment tax rate of 7.9 percent. Added yearly payroll tax collections come to an estimated $142 million. The same calculations are made for

TABLE 6
ACTUAL AND CALCULATED LABOR FORCE PARTICIPATION
(percent)

	Men			Women		
Age	Actual	Calculated	Deviation	Actual	Calculated	Deviation
65	47.1	45.5	+1.6	22.0	20.5	+1.5
66	41.9	42.1	−0.2	18.8	18.8	0.0
67	38.6	38.7	−0.1	17.0	17.1	−0.1
68	35.4	35.3	+0.1	14.7	15.4	−0.7
69	31.5	31.9	−0.4	12.9	13.7	−0.8
70	26.9	28.5	−1.6	11.1	12.0	−0.9
71	24.6	25.1	−0.5	9.8	10.3	−0.5
72	22.1	21.7	+0.4	9.1	8.6	+0.5
73	19.8	18.3	+1.5	7.8	6.9	+0.9

SOURCE: Table 5 in Chapter 5, and author's calculations.

TABLE 7

ESTIMATED ADDITIONAL LABOR FORCE PARTICIPATION (LFP)

	Men			Women		
Age	Population July 1, 1976[a] (thousands)	Added LFP Rate[b] (percent)	Added Workers[c]	Population July 1, 1976[a] (thousands)	Added LFP Rate[b] (percent)	Added Workers[c]
65	794	3.8	30,172	962	2.9	27,898
66	802	3.4	27,268	991	2.4	23,784
67	735	3.1	22,785	937	2.2	20,614
68	697	2.8	19,516	900	1.9	17,100
69	635	2.5	15,875	829	1.7	14,093
70	595	2.2	13,090	786	1.4	11,004
71	554	2.0	11,080	742	1.3	9,646
72	504	1.8	9,072	684	1.2	8,208
73	458	0	0	634	0	0
Total	5,744		148,858			132,347

[a] From U.S. Department of Commerce, Bureau of the Census, *Population Estimates and Projections*, Series P-25, no. 643, issued January 1977, p. 16.
[b] Based on process shown in this appendix.
[c] Population multiplied by estimated added participation rate.

TABLE 8
ESTIMATED ADDITIONAL PAYROLL TAXES FROM MEN

Age	Added Workers[a] (number)	Average Earned Income[b] (dollars)	Added Income[c] (millions of dollars)		Added Tax Collections[d] (millions of dollars)	
			Wages and Salaries	Self-employment	Payrolls	Self-employment
65	30,172	9,000	255	17	29.8	1.3
66	27,268	8,750	224	15	26.2	1.1
67	22,785	8,500	182	12	21.3	0.9
68	19,516	8,250	151	10	17.7	0.8
69	15,875	8,000	119	8	13.9	0.6
70	13,090	7,750	95	6	11.1	0.5
71	11,080	7,500	73	5	8.5	0.4
72	9,072	7,250	62	4	7.3	0.3
73	0	—	—	—	—	—
Total payroll tax					135.8	5.9

[a] See Table 7.
[b] See appendix.
[c] According to Barbara A. Lingg, "Retired-Worker Beneficiaries Affected by the Annual Earnings Test in 1971," *Social Security Bulletin*, vol. 38 (August 1975), 93.9 percent of men work for wages or salaries; 6.1 percent are self-employed.
[d] Taxes figured at 11.7 percent of payrolls and 7.9 percent of self-employment income.

TABLE 9
Estimated Additional Payroll Taxes from Women

Age	Added Workers[a] (number)	Average Earned Income[b] (dollars)	Added Income[c] (millions of dollars)		Added Tax Collections[d] (millions of dollars)	
			Wages and Salaries	Self-employment	Payrolls	Self-employment
65	27,898	7,000	190.8	4.5	22.3	0.4
66	23,784	6,750	156.9	3.7	18.4	0.3
67	20,614	6,500	130.9	3.1	15.3	0.2
68	17,100	6,250	104.4	2.4	12.2	0.2
69	14,093	6,000	82.6	1.9	9.7	0.2
70	11,004	5,750	61.8	1.7	7.2	0.1
71	9,646	5,500	51.8	1.2	6.1	0.1
72	8,208	5,250	42.1	1.0	4.9	0.1
73	0	—	—	—	—	—
Total payroll tax					96.1	1.6

[a] See Table 7.
[b] See appendix.
[c] According to Barbara A. Lingg, "Retired-Worker Beneficiaries Affected by the Annual Earnings Test in 1971," *Social Security Bulletin*, vol. 38 (August 1975), 97.7 percent of women work for wages and salaries; 2.3 percent are self-employed.
[d] Taxes figured at 11.7 percent of payrolls and 7.9 percent of self-employment income.

TABLE 10

ESTIMATED ADDITIONAL INCOME TAXES FROM MEN AND WOMEN

Age	Men			Women		
	Added Workers[a] (number)	Income Tax per Worker[b] (dollars)	Total Income Tax[c] (millions of dollars)	Added Workers[a] (number)	Income Tax per Worker[b] (dollars)	Total Income Tax[c] (millions of dollars)
65	30,172	1,059	32.0	27,898	685	19.1
66	27,268	1,002	27.3	23,784	646	15.4
67	22,785	958	21.8	20,614	597	12.3
68	19,516	914	17.8	17,100	553	9.5
69	15,875	870	13.8	14,093	512	7.2
70	13,090	826	10.8	11,004	463	5.1
71	11,080	771	8.5	9,646	418	4.0
72	9,072	727	6.6	8,208	377	3.1
73	0	—	—	0	—	—
Total income tax			138.6			75.7

[a] See Table 7.
[b] Based on assumption that all workers of a particular age earn average for that wage as shown in Tables 8 and 9, file a separate return as a married person, have no other income to change tax bracket, and take standard deduction plus two dependency deductions for being sixty-five and over.
[c] Estimated added workers multiplied by estimated income tax per worker.

women in Table 9, using lower income data and a lower percentage of self-employment. Added payroll tax collections from female employment come to $98 million per year.

Estimated additional federal income tax collections are shown in Table 10 for both men and women. The total of $214 million is somewhat lower than added payroll tax collections. For men, however, the income tax collections are slightly higher than payroll tax collections while for women the payroll taxes are higher, reflecting their greater regressiveness.